Book of Invocations

Jenny Toupin

Getting Started 1

Protection, Binding & Banishment 12

Chakras.. 19

Essence Magick.. 23

Glamour Magick 29

Spirit Guides 32

Libation, Devotion & Prayer.. 37

Celtic Deities... 39

Greek Deities... 51

Grigori 65

Egyptian Deities 75

Hindu Deities 85

Mesopotamian Deities... 93

Miscellaneous.. 103

Nordic Deities 109

Roman Deities... 117

Saints.. 127

Shinto 135

Slavic.. 143

Getting Started

"An essential portion of any artist's labor is not creation so much as invocation. Part of the work cannot be made, it must be received; and we cannot have this gift except, perhaps, by supplication, by courting, by creating within ourselves that 'begging bowl' to which the gift is drawn." - Lewis Hyde

In science we learn that matter cannot be created nor destroyed. The same concept is applied to magic. Magic is not exclusive to the divine; it is all around us — a well of energy waiting to be tapped into. The way a witch controls magic is an art. That is why we often refer to magic as the craft. There is magic in life, death, beauty, and sorrow. Life is truly a gift. Therefore, we do not create magic, we invoke it. We live it, breathe it, abide by it.

A great professor once taught me not to fret about situations over which I have no control. I am individually responsible for my actions and perceptions. No person can make me feel a certain way. I am responsible for my interpretations and coping mechanisms. Similarly, in your craft, you are responsible. If you believe there are consequences or justifications for your spells, you have that control. True magic isn't far-fetched trickery or sleight of hand. It is a psychological intent igniting a change into the physical world.

This is by no means an introductory book on writing for the craft. While I would never turn away a beginner or novice practitioner, the invocations in this book should be performed by the advanced weaver. There is no shortcut to working with deities. It is more than just picking

1

a name and asking for luck or love. There must be prayer, libation, celebration and meditation with your deities. You know that one friend who only contacts you if they need something? Don't be that follower. If you are comfortable with your practice and your gods, please continue on to my personal book of invocations.

Labels in the craft are only used to differentiate one belief from another, and as similar as paths may seem, no two witches are alike. Whether you are hereditary or starting a new generation of witches, most witches are eclectic. There are those who interpret old traditions into a modern framework, those who stick to strict guidelines of ancient ways and lore, and then the most common practice of combination.

In this introduction, we will discuss the roots of words, clear up misconceptions, and get your ritual space prepared for an invocation. First, let us make clear the difference between being a witch versus being a Pagan. Witchcraft and magic are paths and methods Pagans use, but you do not have to identify as Pagan to practice such methods. Paganism is a broad-spectrum religion; the term is used as an umbrella concept for many different beliefs, similarly to how we categorize Christianity. The following passages are written from the perspective of a Pagan who also practices magic.

You will notice that I reference the dictionary to break down words for explanation. I do this to point out bias and discrepancy, and to widen perspective. For example, let's break down the word 'witch.' These are our options for identity according to www.dictionary.com:

a person, now especially a woman, who professes or is supposed to practice magic or sorcery; a sorceress.

a woman who is supposed to have evil or wicked magical powers: witches in black robes and pointed hats.

an ugly or mean old woman; hag: the old witch who used to own this building.

A witch can be male or female. Male witches are not wizards from Harry Potter or warlocks from Scooby-Doo. Female witches are not ugly, evil old women, though this is exactly how Hollywood represents them. This is why the stigma exists, influenced by a fear instilled thousands of years ago by the flood of Christianity.

Side Note: I have a friend that legitimately compared my beliefs to Harry Potter and thought I believed I was a wizard like the characters in the books. No, I'm not kidding.
Update: She's now studying the path and will be mad at me for calling her out.

Often, I will refer to magic as magick, which is the same thing, just a term coined by the infamous Aleister Crowley to differentiate between magician trickery and magic in a spiritual sense.

Magic (noun) [Defined by Merriam Webster]
1a : the use of means (such as charms or spells) believed to have supernatural power over natural forces
b : magic rites or incantations
2a : an extraordinary power or influence seemingly from a supernatural source
Both pitchers, although they are older, haven't lost their magic.
b : something that seems to cast a spell : ENCHANTMENT
all the mystery, magic and romance which belong to royalty alone
— J. E. P. Grigg
3 : the art of producing illusions by sleight of hand
entertained with acts of jugglery and magic

Merriam Webster does a decent job of explaining magic without any cultural bias. Point three may not seem relevant, but illusion is not just used by magicians; it is also used by those who practice glamour magick. Digging deeper into etymology, you will find that the three wise men, from a common Christian myth you may know, were first referred to as the magus, which we know is in reference to the Persian word for 'Sorcerer' or 'Person of Magic.' There was a time when magick wasn't exclusive to witchcraft. It was a miracle. I disagree that magick is supernatural and will argue that it is a natural force of nature. We witches have laws that govern its flow. We are not opposed to scientific reasoning. Magick is the use of energy, even if science hasn't yet acknowledged the transmission of energy through spiritual means.

3

Is it necessary to call upon a deity when performing magick or a ritual? No. There are different phases of power you can draw upon internally and externally that will be discussed further within this book. You can evoke power from within you and around you, or you can invoke a deity or spirit. Invoking is often related to conjuring. There is not much difference between evocation and invocation, other than invocation is at a higher level and to a greater extent. Conjuration is the direct result of your evocation and invocation, and is both a physical and mental manifestation. Think of invoking like you're 'inviting' someone to your circle, while conjuring is to 'coincide.'

I will not claim to be all-knowing of every god and goddess. I simply write through them from my own experiences and perspective. Remember, you're responsible for your own craft. Your gnosis is just as important as studying from others. Gnosis is a collection of learned experiences on your path that you did not gather from another source.

The following invocations can be easily substituted for many pantheons and parallels. There is no right way or wrong way to speak to the gods if you are respectful and speaking from your heart. My preference is to speak in language I feel the respective god/goddess would prefer. In some cases, it is as if the gods are writing through me and the words are not my own. Some refer to this ability as automatic writing and use it towards divination. Pen hits paper in a way that in other contexts it would not, and so forth.

Much modern practice focuses on a loving goddess and loyal god figure. While there are many negative connotations of a dark god or goddess, there is no shame in following those aspects. To practice any craft, there must be a balance and understanding of all aspects. Light does not always equate to good, as dark does not always equate to evil.

Traditional craft gives a taste of more ancient beliefs. While yes, there are loving god and goddess figures in the craft, ancient rule was held by dark goddesses and gods of war. They were teachers, warriors and beings of great title, strength and honor. With fear of rejection of our modern-day faith, these dark roots were shadowed by the light half of Paganism. Blood witches and those who delve deeper than the surface will practice the ancient ways of the craft.

There is nothing wrong with being unsure of which primary to follow, though in my experience chants and prayer are much more potent when calling out a name. Chills will travel down your spine. The flames of your candles may grow or falter. The temperature may rise or fall drastically. When invoking a particularly powerful deity or multiple deities simultaneously, one may experience vertigo and nausea from the encounter.

If you have not had these experiences, don't be discouraged. Maybe you simply haven't found a deity to connect with, or it may be that you cannot focus. I started off my journey on my magickal path praising Nyx and Erebus as my primaries and had many interesting experiences, but none of them were mind-blowing. It wasn't until many years later that I received signs from Nyx to call to Hekate. Since then, my spell power has amplified and I have had trifold the experiences. Being a Pagan is more than just worshiping a god and magick. It is a constant path of learning and enlightenment. Also remember, some of the unpopular or forgotten gods and goddesses still need prayer. Do not forget the tales that have guided you on your journey and the names that are not as quick to your lips.

Paganism and witchcraft have had a bad reputation for a long time. They are only now more widely accepted because of the loving goddess based teachings of the new-age era. Modern practice usually involves one god and one goddess, parallels and/or opposites meant to represent the divine masculine and divine feminine, respectively. For example, a goddess of the moon and god of the sun. This was taken from a wide variety of pre-existing beliefs, and consolidated into a simpler format. Celebrations of the rule of these primary deities change with the seasons, as their stories reflect the changes within the year, the cycle of life, death and life again.

With that being said, some deities may be more likely to respond in their correlating season. This holds true with spirits, dryads, fae, elves, nymphs and sprites of the land. In addition, communication with a deity will most likely not happen the first time you try to speak to them. If the deity does not seek you, and you seek them, then there must be a bond created. That isn't to say that there isn't a process if they seek you. In my experience, I have had to undergo trials when a deity has reached out to me.

A sign from the Morrigan may be a murder of crows shadowing you throughout your day. A trial of Hekate could be a major life obstacle put before you, to see how well you can handle struggle. A sign of Bast could be a feline choosing you to have a familiar bond. Similar occurrences will start happening more frequently when a god or goddess is trying to reach out to you. There is coincidence and wanting communication, and then there is actually receiving feedback. Be careful not to get those confused and be caught up in the moment. Signs will come when you least expect them, and probably not from the deity you expect.

When invoking a deity, there must be a bond and desire to strengthen that bond. The purpose of invocation is not to achieve power and earthly desires. It is a gift to have your true self be one with the divine. It is the strength in your spine, the tingling in your fingertips, the heat boiling from your blood and glowing on the surface.

There are several ways to categorize the invocations which are used in this text. We all have needs and wants, and some deities are more apt than others for specific subjects. For example, Aphrodite would not only be called upon for beauty, but also to clear one's conscience or negativity. Aphrodite being the daughter of Poseidon, the god of the sea, we would look at the element water. Water is a cleansing and healing element. For a mundane example, this is why we feel refreshed after a shower and rejuvenated after a cold glass of water on a summer day. Water is the source of all life on Earth, thus why we could call on a deity whose element is water for cleansing, healing and even mental healing such as relief from depression. You wouldn't call upon Aphrodite for assistance with bringing someone to justice or for good luck.

So keep in mind which god you choose to speak with and be sure their abilities pertain to your desire for the spell. Another word of advice is to do the mundane work yourself. To find a solution, you must seek one. And if you do not try to seek answers within yourself, no god or goddess will help you. As with any spell, invocation is a combination of internal forces, external forces (such as environmental factors) and divinity or spirituality. Relying on just one of those factors is not a complete spell.

Let's break down the factors of a spell and see why we must combine them: Using just the divine as a source of change is prayer. Using only external factors (such as the environment) is meditation. Lastly, using internal sources to provoke change is motivation, to put it simply. While non-Pagan witches don't use divinity, it is a crucial element to Pagans in forming magick at its most potent.

I would say that most eclectic witches take magick with a grain of salt in their spell-workings, and only combine meditation and motivation to ignite a psychological change. From a cognitive school of thought, this makes sense. Some even believe that the divine factor is symbolic and do not believe in the deities as actual manifestations. This is what separates faith from science: the inability to prove the existence of divine interference.

So I encourage everyone to test this trifold method and come up with their own theories. Perform your spells with and without the divine aspect and note if there are any differences. We can test, hypothesize, and study correlations, but at this point in time we have no solid theories or explanations on the process of spells and their effect on the external environment.

Now, let's look at the definitions of a spell. I am sure you have not noticed before, but the verb (to spell) is taken from the noun (to cast a spell). Here is the Merriam-Webster definition of 'spell,' in the form we are studying:

Spell (Noun)
1a : a spoken word or form of words held to have magic power
b : a state of enchantment
2: a strong compelling influence or attraction

Now compare that with the examples from the Oxford Dictionary:

Spell (Verb) spelled, spelt
[WITH OBJECT]
1 Write or name the letters that form (a word) in correct sequence.
'Dolly spelled her name'
no object 'journals have a house style about how to spell'

More example sentences
1.1 (of letters) make up or form (a word)
'the letters spell the word 'how''

More example sentences
2 Be a sign or characteristic of.
'she had the chic, efficient look that spells Milan'
2.1 Mean or have as a result.
  'the plans would spell disaster for the economy'

Here is my version:
Spell (Verb) – To compose by using a sequence of letters, words and/or symbols to create a pattern
Spell (Noun) – A written composition which uses a sequence of letters, words and/or symbols to create a pattern

Do you see the pattern? Spell a word. Not what you thought of as a spell? There is much stigma not only with the term witchcraft, but also with the words associated with it. Though as you can see above, the etymology shows that the roots are not as abnormal as they are perceived to be.

Within sacred teachings, ancient practices and mythology, there is a series of patterns. Understanding those patterns and accepting the similarities in the beliefs of our fellow Pagans, as well as our brothers and sisters in modern religion, will create a more enriching path.

The divine masculine and divine feminine are sacred symbols that are practiced today in neo-Paganism, usually with a belief in chthonic gods and katabasis. Katabasis is a narrative or ritual in which the person/deity travels to the underworld to learn something, then comes back as if re-born. Chthonic relates to the concept of the underworld. Hell. Whatever you want to call it. Think of Persephone, Lilith and Inanna. The seasonal deities are praised usually as a creation myth told in relation to death and rebirth, like the seasons.

While a lot of Olympian gods have been cast aside in favor of popular deities such as Diana, Hekate, etc., there is an abundance of documentation available on how the old ones were studied, based upon the stories of epic heroes and ancient sources. Great resources can be found on www.ancient-texts.com and www.theoi.com.

Most modern books draw original content from sources like *The Chaldean Oracles, The Odyssey* and even a more modern gem, *Aradia: Gospel of Witches*. The inspiration for this book was derived from The *Hymns of Orpheus*; I had a desire to create a modern interpretation for more than just the Greek pantheon.

Other than that, all we have to turn to are the skewed fragments of Paganism which Christianity carried over, and the teachings of those who claim to pass down the craft as a birthright. And as much as family and oral traditions are preferred, they are very far and few between, and considered a blessing among the community. So I encourage those who practice today to do your research and study actual sources. Look to the people who practiced the worship of our gods back before it was considered witchcraft.

Just as important as the credible sources of our ancient ancestors is the personal spiritual journey within us all that comes through gnosis. Just like the tales of epic heroes from the past and stories of how our gods and goddesses came to be, we can make our own stories. The most important teachings in the craft come from experience.

As a practitioner of traditional craft, I strongly believe there was meaning to how things used to be done, but that does not mean there is no room for improvement. We live in an era of logic and reason, and more recently, enlightenment. The new fad for Pagans and non-Pagans alike seems to be to try to 'awaken' your inner self. Being 'woke' is a term that is commonly used. As humans, we are reluctant to change by nature, though at the same time it fascinates us and encourages us to find meaning and purpose. Whatever the reason that spells work, that we experience magick, there are many who can vouch that it is very much real.

Although not necessary for most traditional paths, I will first include my call to the elements. This is not my only one, and I suggest you write your own to give it personal touches. This should be something coming naturally from your spirit, not a struggle to memorize. Every path is different; with mine I do not call directions because I feel they are irrelevant to my geographical nature. Instead, I like to use items that are symbolic to the element I am calling. For air I use incense, for water a chalice or scrying bowl, for fire a red stone or candle, and for earth a plant or branch of sorts, depending what ritual I will be performing after. Though again, calling elements into your round is purely preference and is not required for any further invocations.

The Dark Quarters

Modest breeze, be free to be
Carry these words and walk the wisp
Tease the tree & move the sea
Tell I will all, the tale of this mist
Air, I welcome ye

Bend my blood, control my beast
Feel the flood & feed the weak
Waves of woe will wash away
The hidden they seek to cast to grey
Water, I welcome ye

Sear the seal that holds thy power
Bind this bond with heat of blood
Come stand proud & glow with honor
Passion burns & that it should
Fire, I welcome ye

Douse the dirt where death may grow
Fill the void and veer of weeds
Share the secrets of what's below
Loud I'll sing and laud thy rede
Earth, I welcome ye

Praise the Day which keeps Night warm
Pay the debt to keep thy strength
Heed the flower, taste the thorn
Hail the bane, and serve the horn

Welcome Lady, hear my plea
Will is fading, help my need

Body offered, blood I drink
Hear thy daughter, bite the brink

Taken beneath the darkest wing
Bide the left and enter my dreams
I embrace ye Lady in my circle
Blessed be the might of her will

Protection, Binding & Banishment

Also highly recommended is the following chant (or similar) to maintain homeostasis. When invoking a deity, anything could happen. Nothing is more important than your safety, physical and mental. Whether left hand or right, there always must be a balance, or at least an acknowledgment of such. The following chant is quick and easy to help meditate to ground oneself before an invocation. If you sway more one way or another, you could feel ill or weak, and the ritual could have effects long after, especially when tampering with dark arts. Balance is essential and balance is protection.

"It reminds us that we are indeed a product of our decisions, not our circumstances." - Stephen Covey

Balance

I call upon thy lighter half
To aid me with this right hand craft
May the balance not be broken
By these words that I have spoken
Awaken.

I call upon thy darker half
To aid me with this left hand craft
May the balance not be broken
By these words that I have spoken
Awaken.

Even with much preparation, the unexpected always lurks. If you summon a spirit you had no intention of calling or another energy leaks into your workings, you must be prepared to react, and to react quickly. So below, I will include precautions you can take, and a spell for banishment. Banishment can be as simple as standing your ground and speaking firmly to the spirit. Though depending on what is drawn from the other side, some are peskier to get rid of.

Along with chant and intent, there are some useful items to keep near where you cast your round. For those adept in herbs, here is a list of those which are for purification, protection and cleansing. They could also be used for banishment. You can burn them as incense over charcoal, sprinkle them within your circle, cleanse with them via ritual bath, use them as oil if prepared prior, and some you can even ingest, such as in a tea. Though if unfamiliar with baneful herbs, do not assume or guess that one is safe to ingest.

Herb List:

Acacia
Angelica
Balm of Gilead
Barley
Basil
Black Cohosh
Blood Root
Cactus
Caraway Seeds
Catnip
Cinnamon
Clove
Elder Flowers
Mandrake
Marshmallow
May Apple
Myrtle
Pipsissewa
Rattlesnake Root

For those not savvy in herbalism, there are other tools which can be used to protect yourself from unwanted spirits or banes. If using crystals, you want those which absorb both pure and negative energy. As mentioned earlier, balance is key. These stones can be placed within your round, worn as jewelry or even used to make essential oils. Even just transferring your energy into these stones will work fine. Use stones such as, but not limited to, the following.

Crystal List:

Agate
Amber
Clear quartz
Fluorite
Hematite (Hematite rings work wonders and are sold at most metaphysical shops.)
Labradorite
Malachite
Moon Stone
Obsidian (Snowflake or standard)
Onyx
Smoky quartz
Tiger's eye
Tourmaline

Banishing Chant

I cast ye back
To where ye hail
To swamps of black
And leave no trail

I banish ye
Leave this place
Away from me
Leave no trace

Sleep in peace
Away from here
Shadows cease
And darkness clear

Heed this warning: Be careful what you wish for.
Cliché, I know. Be careful what you play with. Those comfortable in
the dark arts may not want to banish a negative spirit, but will instead
consider it a lucky find. Though not everyone believes in the three-fold,
I think there is a common understanding of karma, and of leaving that
alone which has ill intent. I had to pay the price of darkness when I first
started and had no one to warn me of the consequences. This is my
warning to you. There must be an equal sacrifice for what you intend to
change. You must be justified. Balance.

If a negative entity attaches itself to you and you wish to use it to your
benefit, you must have something to offer in return. You may be a
witch, but you are not a god. Below I will include a spell for binding.
Use it how you wish, but know it can be used to control a spirit or
energy against its will. Often when one hears of binding in new-age
practice, we think of protection or an 80's witch film. Let's look at
some of the relevant definitions from Webster's dictionary to get a
better understanding of the different ways of binding.

Definition of bind
bound play \ˈbaṅd\; binding
Transitive & Intransitive Verb

1. to exert a restraining or compelling effect - a promise that binds
2. to become hindered from free operation - Rust caused the door to
bind in its frame.
3. to cause to have an emotional attachment - the emotional ties that
bind us
4. to put under an obligation - binds himself with an oath
5. to make secure by tying - His hands were bound with rope.
6. to confine, restrain, or restrict as if with bonds - ... she was not
wholly bound in mind by her middle-class existence

All of these definitions can be justified. As for restraints, we will not
use physical ones, though we may use a physical object to symbolize

something we wish to bind. We don't necessarily make the binding secure by tying an actual rope, but we do seal the spell. You may still use rope, ribbon or string as symbolism upon an object during the spell. To seal could be to tie a knot, cut it, burn it or bury it.

Do NOT bind something with ill intent to yourself. What does work is binding an energy to a specific object. You are probably familiar with binding protective energy to your tools and charms, and you can do the same with negative energy. I suggest making a poppet especially for the use of binding. If bound to an object, it can be used for later purposes.

The energy bound does not necessarily have to be good or negative energy. It could simply be your own spell power to be saved for later use, or even given to another trusted practitioner to aid in their work. Below is a spell used for binding.

Supplies: 1 poppet, 1 red string/twine

Chant while wrapping the poppet in twine:

I bind thee, spirit
From doing me harm
I condemn thee with
My witch's charm (Tie your first knot, keep wrapping the twine.)

Your power now mine
And to this poppet
Your will I do bind
You cannot stop it (Tie your second knot, keep wrapping the twine.)
By power of three
And all that be
You work for me
So mote it be (Tie your third and final knot.)

Some may be skeptical about the true power of invocations and would argue that the words do not matter, only intent. But the words very much aid in this factor and help with our visualization, which of course leads to manifestation. Take a mantra for example: in a way still poetic, but short and to the point. This repetition promotes someone to visualize what they are speaking of, often with themselves at the center of success, health or whatever the mantra is set to attain.

Poetry has been used for centuries alongside song and dance to induce a mystical state. For example, saying, 'Goddess, please let me pass that exam tomorrow,' has quite a different effect than saying something like this: 'I invoke thee Athena, woman of wisdom, and she of the arts. Expand my aura, lit through a prism, and shone through my heart. May memory not falter. May my mind maintain. My mind is my altar. This knowledge is my domain.' Saying both of those statements aloud, which has the greater personal effect? One seems more like begging, while the latter is more about taking control and owning personal knowledge. One of the key factors of being successful in your magick is confidence. But there should also be a level of respect when approaching a god or goddess.

To ensure protection, maintain control. Do not foolishly offer your body as medium or consort to an unknown entity. Be strong when performing your arts and keep utmost confidence. Your energy is a direct reflection of your mood. We can hone energies, as you will learn in the next section, but you must be aware of how your composure affects your energy. Even if you cannot see energy in color, think of it like an aura. There are other senses you can use to identify the aura such as touch, hearing, smell, intuition, or the gift of knowing. You have internal energy that I refer to as 'chakra,' but let's separate the external as 'aura.' Chakra will be your nature and aura will be your demeanor.

At homeostasis, your chakras should be balanced at all times. The only time in which they are not is if you intentionally make it so. Unbalanced chakras will throw off your aura as well as your physical health, potentially. You can heal your chakras to change your aura, but you cannot switch the two around. The auras are the colors of life. You have them, as does every creature around you. There is a great deal of psychology that can be viewed from auras, as well as physical health. You may see these auras in layers around someone, each representing a certain characteristic, whether it be emotion, health or spirit.

We will continue evaluating aura through color to make it easier. As Pagans, we integrate the use of color into almost all of our workings, whether it be through candles, crystals or, now, auras. The only difference with auras is how you sense and perceive the colors. For example, a bright yellow is a creature displaying happiness and honesty, while a dull yellow could be apathy, frustration, or even sickness.

Please read on to the next section to see how to balance chakras. This is the best way to tackle unwanted auras and to start healing within yourself before seeking help from others. Remember, if your aura is dull or dark, you may be more susceptible to bad energy or negative spiritual forces.

Chakras

Now that we have gone through the importance of wording and confidence, we will briefly touch on other factors that will reinforce your spoken invocations. There are many different philosophies on meditation, though the method that I am sure comes to mind is Buddhist meditation. Even if you don't agree with their mythology and deities, their meditation techniques seriously work. To put this simply, think of your chakras as a symbolic way to help channel the energies specific to certain areas of the body. This is a visual aid similar to a specific crystal or candle. The color-coding and associations work in the same manner.

I will go through this type of meditation step by step for those that are unaware of how it works. If you are familiar, feel free to skim over. However, I would suggest a refresher, as this type of meditation has proven to greatly assist in traveling to the astral plane and in separating the spirit from the flesh. This is done before every circle cast to purify yourself and your energy, and to put focus towards the nature of your intent.

To start off, sit with your legs crossed in front of your altar or sacred space. This could be an empty room, out in the middle of the woods or a faerie ring. Find a place that brings you peace and in which you will have no distractions. Be in a space where you can sit comfortably with your eyes closed, away from harsh light. To utilize this technique to the fullest, be sure to keep an erect posture and practice proper breathing techniques. Yes — breathing. With every inhale and exhale, breathe in deeply from your diaphragmatic region and feel the flow of energy rise from your waist, referred to as the sacral area, through the solar plexus, the heart, the throat, until finally you are in full exhale.

As mentioned previously, during this exercise we will use color association to channel your energies, or chakras. First, we look at the root chakra, associated with the color red and located in your lumbar (back) region. This is where we hold in aggression and passion. Ever hear of the expression 'grow some backbone'? Each of the seven chakras are of equal importance, but this is the one that grounds us. This internal vibration flows through the base of your spine, and the vibrational frequency extends through your legs and feet. This chakra taps into our amygdala and keeps balance with the need for survival and the stress response.

Still maintaining those breathing techniques, with your eyes closed, start to picture a red aura glowing from the base of your spine. With each inhale, see the vibrancy of the red light breathing in with you and expanding as you exhale. Stay focused on this chakra for a moment, and grow the light appropriately within your subconscious. Feel the power surging, almost as an emotional high. Don't stay in one state for too long, because the key to this meditation is balance. Though, you can take some time to play with this new-found control. Practice increasing and decreasing the size of your root chakra. How does it make you feel? After a few minutes or so of feeling your backbone, so to speak, we move onto the chakra called the sacral (navel) chakra.

The sacral chakra is in your lower abdomen and controls emotional response. Think of this energy as orange. It controls desire and imagination. Still working on our limbic system, start to visualize an orange glowing light, similar to the red one. This will stem from the navel region around the areas of the kidneys, bladder and reproductive system. This energy should evoke pleasure and maybe even a sensual response.

Keep the balance of your root chakra active and at a controllable size. Try keeping your root chakra the same size while simultaneously playing with the sacral chakra. Feel the flow of emotional energy and determination. After you are done experimenting and controlling the capacity of this energy, align the two chakras, so they are the same size, brightness and intensity.

Subsequent to the naval chakra is the solar plexus. Ever hear of the expression of a 'gut feeling'? This energy is referred to as the source of power. This energy also subconsciously elicits behavior. Think of this as your 'conscience.' Go ahead and start to visualize a yellow glowing light in your stomach area. This chakra sends direct messages to your third eye and develops your personal intuition. You should be feeling extreme sensitivity, a warmness that resembles the sun and happiness. Think of it like an electric jolt of power. Again, while synchronizing the other two chakras, master expanding and decreasing the solar plexus chakra.

While still preserving the first three chakras, let's move on to the heart chakra. This chakra not only affects the heart, but the entire circulatory system and upper extremities as well. This energy promotes purification, peace and compassion. When perfecting the balance in this chakra, it helps to drive away the negativities held within your other chakra regions. This is where the awakening begins and self-love and empathy flourish. Visualize this energy as a glowing, green sphere. It feels like the essence of spring, friendship and wisdom.

Next is the thoracic chakra, or the throat chakra. This is the energy of truth, healing and mending bonds. Think of this blue light as an ocean wave splashing upon you. This is the chakra of cleansing and re-birth. This projects your desires and feelings into expression and communication. By now, the multitude of different energies may be becoming more difficult to maintain. Take this process slowly.

Keeping balance with the lower chakras, we move on to the third eye, the most talked-about chakra. This is the energy of psychic power and intuition. The equivalent to mastering this chakra would be sitting on top of Maslow's Hierarchy of Needs. This energy is mindful and works on focus. Picture this chakra as purple, though notice how hard it is to expand this light in your mind. Do not force this chakra to expand too much, as you may be going beyond your ability and nature. The more you practice, the easier this will be. Another variance to this state would be 'The Dreaming.'

Lastly, we have the crown. Envision this light to resemble a halo above your head. The color should be white and twinkling, like a crown of stars. This is beyond the power and needs of self; it is more an enlightenment for greater purpose. This chakra focuses on external influence as opposed to the previous six chakras. This force connects your being with the divine.

Even as complex as this meditation is, there is still so much more you can add. Once you have tried this technique a few times, try adding more senses in, such as smell and taste. This will amplify your energy further. Use this guide before calling the elements into your circle. Amplify corresponding energies. Within your rite, one day you will be able to magnify your chakras corresponding to the purpose of your spell. I have found this to be much more effective than simply relying on using the minor energies emitted from receptive/projective hands. While it is useful to move the source of power in a concentrated direction, shouldn't you make sure you're tapping into the correct ley line first?

Essence Magick

Now let's talk about the taboo. If this is not your first read about the craft, I'm sure you know all about light magick, an ye harm none, and the three-fold. That is great, and I deeply respect Wiccans and their Rede. However, this next section would be considered taboo by Wiccans, as it goes against that Rede. 'An ye harm none, do what ye will' does not just refer to others, but also to self.

Here is where we discuss the potency of blood magick and sex magick, among other different workings with bodily essence. Having imagery of who your spell is for is one thing, but having their essence, or your own magickal essence, incorporated into your craft will amplify the effect exponentially. I will advise never to obtain essence without permission of another person, and to make sure they are aware of and consent to any working you may do. Of course, judgement is always yours. Most often, someone will reach out to you.

When we talk about blood magick, we are not asking you to sacrifice your first born, kill anything or anyone or even hurt yourself. Essence magick is very potent, and small quantities are needed, no matter what you are doing. There are also appropriate times to use essence magick, and inappropriate times. Think of essence also as a higher quality offering.

A really great suggestion comes from Raven Grimassi in his book *Grimoire of the Thorn-Blooded Witch*. In his book, he focused on working with blood as well as plant essence. It's a great read, even if just for the inspiration for building your own path. I will let you delve into that book on your own if you find it interesting. Below, I will share with you my path and experiences in using blood magick.

Blood magick and any essence magick pairs well with the use of sacred symbols within your work. By sacred symbols, I mean using structures like runes, Ogham or Theban. A simple way to combine these methods is to use a pillar candle (the color of which denotes the type of spell you're casting), a ceremonial dagger to carve the sacred symbol or name on the bottom or base, and a few drops of blood.

Other essences work in a similar manner. While blood works in most cases, for workings with love and passion you may want to use other fluids, to put it appropriately. To those who have never done this, sex magick is nothing to be squeamish about. It is natural and is symbolic of life itself. Essence is not something you can store for long periods of time, but can be prepped before a ritual. Though I know some that even create essence during a ritual, like some followers of Lilith.

Other less common essences can include sweat, tears and saliva. I have learnt that saliva can be a good replacement for blood in a ritual, though I personally have not tried this. Below, I will give an example of essence magick. You can include similar additions to your invocation rites for a more potent effect.

Banishing

Tools: black candle, white candle, ceremonial dagger, finger prick

I used this to banish negative energy surrounding a friend who was having a period of bad luck, surviving abuse and an attempted suicide. I used a female-formed black candle, but a pillar will suffice. Use the ceremonial dagger to carve the name of the individual that needs a negative energy banished. If you are clearing negative energy from a place, simply use sacred symbols or carve 'evil' into the bottom of the candle. On the white candle, carve the same name, and also a symbol of light magick or peace. Draw a pentagram, Celtic cross or ankh, if nothing else.

Put the two candles side by side. If you have a representation of this person, you can put that in the center. The black candle should always be on the left, and the white candle should always be on the right. Place the ceremonial dagger in front of the candles, laying it horizontally. Take a moment to practice breathing techniques, meditate and call upon balance as suggested in the previous section. Prick a finger from your projective hand and smear the blood on the sacred symbols and names under both of the candles. It is very important to use the projective hand, as we do not want to take in any external energy just yet.

Light the black candle and chant the following, focusing on the negative energy leaving your friend and going into your receiving hand. I want you to visualize a thick black fog being expelled from this person's body and into the palm of your hand. Hold your palm straight forward toward the black candle. Chant the following:

Shrouded shade
I expel you
Vile villain
I extract you
Dark drifter
I banish you

By the power of good and light
I take you into me this night
Leave my friend, unhinge your chains
Begone as I end her pain

Once all of the negative energy has been absorbed, it is time to banish the entity. Erase your friend from your thoughts so the evil may not creep back in. You will know this works if you feel a choking feeling while holding the energy. You may feel dizzy and disoriented. Stay focused. Chant the following while firmly placing your projective hand to the ground. Visualize the darkness being expelled from your body and into the ground.

I cast out thee evil
And all your heinous ways
I am not your vessel
In the Earth you will stay

I bind thee, Darkness
Banish you below
Damned to the fortress
Of all left hollow

Take a moment to breathe and restore balance. I recommend the balance chant at the beginning of this book and some energy meditation. Picture your friend smiling and glowing with light. It is now time to light the white candle. Channel positive energy from within yourself and hold out your projective hand, to the white candle this time, palm facing forward. Say the following chant:

May love and light come your way
May within your heart it stay
I shield you from Shadow's hold
Keep you well, happy and bold

Let the candles burn all the way down. Afterward, you need to dispose of the remains of the black candle and the dish it was on. You don't want any of that energy to linger if you missed some! As for my experience, after this ritual my friend removed herself from the abusive situation, stopped self-harm, became very social and even fell in love and became engaged.

I will give one more example of blood magick. This time we will use the essence of someone else. Someone very close to me had given me a tincture made with his blood, patchouli, sandalwood and a few other components in case of an emergency. He asked me to hang onto it until it was absolutely necessary. I didn't ask many questions, just took it and hid it away. A witch will know when the time is right!

Later, he was diagnosed with stage two brain cancer, which was rapidly spreading. To put it in perspective, he had a tumor the size of a golf ball. He became distant, suicidal and a physical wreck, especially after chemotherapy. Having poison literally leak from your body when you sweat is debilitating. We started to lose hope when a month later he became stage three. He was given less than a ten percent chance of survival.

Below I will include a spell I used to shrink his tumor and banish the cancer cells. Yes, it could have been coincidence, but it really was a miracle how that golf ball became a microscopic speck!

Disclaimer: Never use holistic remedies or magick in place of doctor-recommended treatment. Use these practices in addition to an existing health plan.

Cancer Healing

Tools: the affected blood tincture, charcoal/resin-based incense, censer, white candle, blue candle, ceremonial dagger, finger prick

Similar to the previous ritual, use your ceremonial dagger to carve a name and, if you choose, a sacred symbol at the bottom of each candle. White symbolizes cleansing and purification, and blue is for physical and emotional healing. It is appropriate to call upon spirit or your preferred lunar god-figure, as well as the element of water or corresponding deity.

Use the finger prick on your projective hand to stamp a small portion of blood on the bottoms of both candles, as well as in your incense base. Chant something like the following while lighting the candles:

The days grow longer
As you grow weak
My hope is stronger
Than the end you seek

I cleanse your body
Your ill thoughts and soul
Your melancholy
And your misery

I shrink your tumor
Until nothing left
By spell and conjure
Your illness now heft

Now light the incense within the censer. Use the tincture of the affected's blood and put some around your incense mixture, atop your blood. Visualize the life being brought back to the affected. Picture the literal tumor shrinking and chant the following:

Cancer begone!
Take your leave
Carry on
Your bane, I cleave

As always, let the candles fully burn. Imagine the negative energy being stripped away. After the incense has burnt out, bury the remains of the tainted incense, and do NOT look back. Make sure to clean your supplies thoroughly. Of course, as with any bodily fluid, be careful when handling.

Glamour Magick

Mentioned lightly in the introduction was glamour magick, that of illusion and trickery. Though that's not the entirety of this practice. It is a social magick, commanded by presence, manipulation, charisma, charm and psychology. Putting on a veil through glamour magick is useful for many things, especially for practical desires such as beauty, mental stamina, or to impress someone, for instance at a job interview.

Through glamour magick, you put on hypothetical rose-colored goggles and make people see what you want them to see. I often use this in conjunction with attraction spells or in workings in which I want attention to shift. Although, you can also use glamour magick for the opposite effect, to repel. A glamour could even be cast to make someone out of sight. No, not invisible – just overlooked.

This technique can be beneficial when working with deities mentioned in this book as a means to mentally prepare for their presence. You want to impress the deity enough to pay attention to you and to be heard, without seeming arrogant or nervous.

This type of spell work is usually simple; no type of intricacy is required. For beauty, I work with Aphrodite. I'll consecrate rose water for her and use some to bless myself. A mirror, even one that isn't dedicated to your sacred space, should be used while stating your desires. Positive affirmations repeated daily while blessing your crown with rose water and giving libation to a deity associated with love, is considered basic glamour magick.

Positive affirmations are statements you make about yourself that maybe you don't find true, but you want to believe. Try repeating something like this every morning in the mirror, firmly looking yourself in the eyes and believing in what you say:

I am beautiful.
I am strong.
I deserve love.
I am powerful.
I am in control of my future.

You may feel silly at first, but trust me, it works! Another good way to carry around a glamour for extended periods of time is to infuse your intent in a trinket. This could be a ring, a knotted bracelet, or even a small satchel with a piece of rose quartz in it. I personally use a necklace that allows me to infuse essential oil into it.

Think of this as a personal libation. You are taking the offering yourself, because you deserve it. You are your own god. You are your goddess. In glamour, you have complete control.

Ritual baths or just simply washing your face can get rid of a glamour when it's no longer needed. Sometimes, glamour magick can be consuming and can turn negative even with the most positive intentions. You don't want to appear over-zealous and cocky *all* the time.

More than just mental preparation, glamour is also all about treating yourself to look your best. You can't be mentally prepared without proper hygiene. Get your hair done, or nails if that's your thing. Maybe treat yourself to a new outfit or makeup.

There is an ethereal and physical mask that exfoliates our magic and the well-being of our minds. Speaking of, a literal facemask is perfect as preparation for a glamour spell. Get all of the negative energy out of you. Nobody has time for that.

This type of magick also has roots to those who practice fae magick. Many cultures paint the fae as mischievous folk that have many faces, in a sense of glamour. Some believe that glamour magick itself was derived from the fae. I mentioned previously that a glamour could be used to make someone "invisible." Well, legends say that's exactly how these mythical creatures keep out of sight.

Much like an aura, those masked by a glamour have a shade to them, a shine or luster. This is a physical warmth in your body as a result of the glamour. I think this is where the expression comes from when people say, "Your skin is glowing!"

Nope. Just a glamour.

Once you are confident, feel your best and look your best, you are ready to conquer anything. Though glamour isn't meant to be a permanent thing. Once you become what was in you all along, you no longer need to do daily spells. Glamour is funny that way. With the power of a big wave crashing upon you, you somehow ignite a fire beneath your feet. When you feel that fire in the midst of rain, you know that the power is in you.

Spirit Guides

Depending on tradition, it is debatable exactly what a spirit guide is, though it is often confused with a familiar. While a familiar can be a spirit, a familiar is bound intentionally through a pact. A spirit guide is and always has been with you. Knowing your spirit guide and having a relationship with them is important for ritual work, especially with invocations. Because what you conjure up isn't always as intended, your spirit guide can help you through and offer guidance and aid with external magick, whether it be with protection, binding or banishment.

A spirit guide may only make themselves known when needed. Even then, their work often goes unnoticed. But if you reach out and make your intentions known that you want a relationship with them, they are more likely to step out of the shadows. There are infinite ways to try to communicate with your spirit guide, but I will give an example through guided meditation.

Before you meditate, write down a list of questions you want to ask your guide. This isn't a meditation you will do all of the time, so it's important that you use your time wisely. It takes a lot of energy to project from your corporeal body.

When you do meet your guide, it is important to ask them their name. If they are ready to work with you, they will tell you. Even if you do see them, they may not speak their name on the first encounter. My guide's name is Mael.

Ask what type of offerings they like. Ask if there's a time of day when it is easiest to speak with them. Ask them about the different ways they manifest. They are a part of you, bonded in the fibers of your being. They are not there to grant you wishes or show you the future. Your purpose here is to build a partnership and to coincide.

Ritual preparation is recommended, although the act itself will be informal. Before you head off on your journey, perform a wash or cleansing. Repeat the balance chant a few times and make sure you are level-headed. Lastly, make sure you are well-rested. We don't want you falling asleep during meditation.

First, you need to attune yourself with nature and block out distractions. Try to find a place out of reach from civilization, where you can't easily hear the sound of cars or run into somebody. I chose a wooded area, but it doesn't have to be. No ritual tools are needed, just your mind, soul and body.

Don't have any expectations set on a particular animal or guide because it's popular. This can alter your meditation and perception. If you want your guide to be a wolf, and you can't stop thinking about wolves, you my feed your brain incorrect information. You don't want to influence or manifest your desire. You want your spirit to connect with its guide. I did this meditation more than once, as this was my mistake the first time.

I was set on having my guide represented as a cat. He actually ended up taking on the form of a sparrow, though not always. Sometimes I see him with the head, wings and talons of a sparrow, but the body of a man, similar to how the Egyptian deities are portrayed.

In the craft, most of us find comfort in nature, and usually have an affinity for a particular element. Feel free to incorporate your senses with the element you feel the strongest association toward. Your spirit guide may also be attuned to your element. Mine is air.

Trust your gut. When you light your ritual candles, is there always a flame that outshines the others? When you call the quarters, does one presence come through stronger? We aren't going to call a circle, but

33

ask your element to protect you. Ask for them to be by your side and guide you where you need to be. Tell them your intentions. Work with the spirits of the land.

When you know, you know. Once you find your perfect space, get comfortable. This process could take a while, so comfort is important. You may lose track of time as this is a deep meditation. I was in astral for over an hour before meeting my guide. Please reference the previous section on meditation to warm up. Astral projection isn't a requirement, but that is the goal.

Astral projection is an out of body experience – a dreamlike state of being. Whenever the soul leaves the body, there is a chance of danger creeping its way in. Focus is of utmost importance. State aloud your intentions. Ask your element to protect you while you are in this meditation. At this time, you should have your chakras under control and balanced as second-nature. If you are struggling to do this, don't move onto the next step until you have control.

When we get to visualization, remember in great detail your surroundings. Take a picture within your mind. And any door you walk through, remember every sliver of wood and every fault. Be mindful of crossroads found in archways and note physical changes with every step.

There are many layers of realms in our world, that the naked eye cannot fathom. There are levels with sub-layers and nooks and crannies you have to be prepared for. Like the famous saying, "As above, so below," be careful where you go. We are in between the realms. It's easy to fall into a place unintentionally.

Now you will practice visualization. I will give you an example of what to envision, but it's alright to let the picture paint a different story the deeper you are in meditation. The goal is for your spirit to leave the plane we are on currently, and travel to one where you can meet your guide. Close your eyes, focus on the colors of your chakras and practice the following breathing techniques.

Inhale deeply. With each inhale, have the colors of your chakras be absorbed inward. Exhale slowly. With each exhale, push the chakras back outward. Do this until you are completely calm. Next when in inhale, do the same, but swirl the colors into a clockwise spiral. When you exhale, picture a counterclockwise spiral.

When you are in complete control, you should be tapped into your soul, or spiritual essence. Inhale and exhale deeply one more time. This time on the exhale, imagine your soul stepping out of your body. What do you see around you? Your surroundings should be the same when standing next to yourself. Take a few steps forward and take note of the changes.

In front of you, you see a door. It's pale oak with black bolts. Vines cover it completely and a calm darkness sleeps around it. Fireflies light your path and urge you to the door. The ground beneath your feet is soft but sturdy. The dirt is obsidian. With each step, ripples form around you as if you are walking across a river.

When you finally reach the door, face your palm toward it and command it open with your spirit. A yellow light leaks through and draws you in. Lush grass is under your feet. The forest speaks. The brook babbles. The light is warm. The wind caresses your cheek. The journey is yours from here.

Like any relationship with a deity, it is important to show the same love to your spirit guide with libation, devotion and prayer. After you connect, you may get a nudge from time to time when you aren't giving them enough attention. Whenever I feel a disconnect from my craft, a sparrow finds my path.

When you start to feel tired or drained, it's time to bring your ethereal self back to the corporeal world. It is best to ask your guide for assistance with this, since this is their realm. If they can't tell you, or if you didn't get a chance to meet them, stay calm. Stay alert.

It is difficult for a witch to lose their spirit when there's magick in their heart. Be confident in your direction. Remember the element that you called to before projection? Call unto them. Ask them to lead a trail back to yourself.

Stay clear of distractions. Don't eat or drink from this plane. Do not grant any favors to strangers. Stay on your path until you reach the open door you came through.

Libation, Devotion & Prayer

After you have made these preparations, you are welcome to dive straight into invocations, though it is recommended to prepare offerings for the deity you plan to work with, or even maintain a shrine. You can decorate your altar or consecrated area. Some people keep separate shrines in their home. Shrines do not have to be elaborate or obvious. They could be a picture above a bookcase, some candles on an end table, and so forth. Shrines are especially useful if you follow a path that doesn't allow you to alter the land for use of rituals, such as burying charms or leaving herbs and salt unswept.

Make your libations personal to the deity you are calling. If calling Hekate, light a lantern or leave a symbol of the crossroads. If Iris, set up a prism or reflective crystal. And lastly, be confident in your chants. While I will not disagree with those who say incantations can be performed without speaking, it will be more effective and beneficial for you to say your words aloud with pride and confidence. Never disrespect deities, but prove to them you want to be heard, and deserve to be heard.

With the suburbs and city life of the modern-day world, we don't all have the option of being out in nature with our rites, so it is alright to bring nature to you. If nature is not abundant in your area, support your local metaphysical shop or connect with your local Pagan council for support. For example, I once sponsored a Pagan community garden in Oakland County, Michigan for families to grow and learn together openly in the community in a positive light, and to share with each other herbs, flowers and food that were usually not available. We are in an age of spiritual awakenings, acceptance and enlightenment. The opportunity should be seized; don't expect someone else to take action! This is a great alternative for an offering to a deity. Keep the environment clean and abundant, and share with your brothers and sisters of the craft. On this path, we prove ourselves with the actions we take to attain the knowledge to act on our problems.

When deliberating upon a gift to a deity, remember the gifts they bring you that may be taken for granted. The trees that give us oxygen, the lakes that hydrate us, the sun that warms us; all of these may seem obvious, but when's the last time you thanked the Earth Mother for a bountiful garden or the Sun King for a bright, gorgeous day? I am vague on names to respect the deities' different aspects and epithets, but all of our cultures have similar stories to share and legends to behold. So, do not fixate on the name if you do not have a specific path. I think we can all agree that magick is everywhere.

The best kind of prayer you can give to a god or goddess is one which doesn't ask for anything in return. An example would be my recent devotion to Hekate, Nyx, Erebus, Isis and Cernunnos (What a spread, right?). I did not find it necessary to do a separate ritual for each, but rather invited them into my compass and asked them to share my bounty, magic and happiness, which they had helped me find. I dedicated trinkets that were charged in their honor, an athame for both Hekate and Isis (as they have been guiding my path for about three years now), as well as stones and a blessing of oil mixed with various prosperous herbs to share my light and good bounty. Candles were lit for Nyx, Erebus and Cernunnos, and thanks were provided. With Winter Solstice coming up, I was sure to give Cernunnos some extra love and care.

Of course, prayer doesn't need to be so intricate, though devotional ceremonies are nice to do every once in a while. I find that most Pagans shy away from the word 'prayer,' like it has already been claimed by dominant faiths. Prayer is not owned by just one god, so please use it for those you follow. More than anything else, prayer is acknowledgment of higher power. It is like reaching out of your physical body to shake hands with your deity. Show respect to those higher powers, especially if you decide to invoke. Spells are more likely to take effect if you practice prayer often.

Celtic Deities

Aengus

Words as smooth as silk
I beg ye, leave my lips

My presence will bring stars
Crashing at my feet
Pestilence of great wars
My keen will defeat

Through you, Aengus
I will speak
Be among us
I decree

Aengus, I invoke ye
Master of poetry

Whisper the windings of the wind
Into my ear
Come forth unto my voice commands
Let me hear

Badb

Fields of death
Fire of wrath
Wars of others
Sons & brothers

Set the siren
For loved ones' pass
Sing the anthem
Through bloodied grass

I hear your voice
Through echoed cries
You are my choice
My soothing guise

Badb, I call to you
Battlefield mistress
And by sacred yew
I embrace your kiss

Come to my shattered field
Take the pain from atop my brow
Take cover with your shield
To you I take a heavy vow

A life of love and love of life
With bravery I face the strife

Brigid

Blessed lady
Of forge and hearth
Good and saintly
Ye warm our hearts

I drink to ye
Thy sweet nectar
Heavenly mead
O' Great Protector

Please take libation
Of drink and coin
And incantations
Witches rejoin
At the ol' oak tree
For victory

Brigid I call to ye
In perfect harmony
Holy healer
Sage and teacher

Please bless us with thy new spring light
Save us from this winter plight

Cerridwen

Above, below and in between
Seer of all, seen and unseen
Hidden knowledge
Come forth to me
I swear and pledge
My loyalty

Cerridwen
Teach us again
Show us the way
Of night and the day

Please come forth, Cerridwen
Witch of the cauldron
Please share your desire
For knowledge and power

By herb and tree
And alchemy
Share with me
The seen and unseen

Cernunnos

Our Father of foundation
Rested in our roots
Green Man and vegetation
Master of the flute

The hunt is in our hearts
His holy hill dominion
Slumbers wint'ry darkness
In wait of resurrection

Cernunnos
O, Horned One
He Beneath the Rose
May you rise
And let the realms unfold

Cernunnos, I invoke ye
Wrap me in your bounty

Rebirth me from your soil
And let the withered spoil

Dagda

God of plenty
God of change
Fruitful trees
As days exchange

Seasons churn
At the sound of your harp
Children yearn;
Hymn and hark

Eochaid, Rśad, of the Tuatha Dé Danann
Ruler of the trench
Betwixt god and man
Mortal and witch

Slayer of the living
Beloved King
Raiser of the dead
Come now, Eochaid

Danu

Mist of magick
Grove of oakwood
By the broomstick
It's understood

She will be there

Mother goddess
Holy empress

The mother
The teacher
The warrior
Please come to us

Queen of the faeries
Flow of the river
Whispers of the trees
She does deliver-

Hope to me

Praise Danu
Lady, thank you
For the heavens, the Earth, the trees
Oh glory, come to me

Lugh

Oh reaper
And keeper
Of pain in our hearts

Oh savior
And seeker
Of skills in the arts

No fear nor tears
Could keep him from
That treasured spear

Oh leader
And speaker
Of Tuatha Dé Danann

I invoke ye
On my journey
To be all that I can be

Morrigan

Crone, the Mother of Earth, the Maiden
Praise the gods and praise the Morrigan
With ways of the old and heart within
The roots of her womb where life began

I call the Crow
The Phantom Queen
Bow aglow
And eyes of green

Goddess of war
Woman of brawn
Lady of lore
Rejoice at dawn

Come now Morrigan
Dance with me
Set foot to the land
Come set us free

Tuatha Dé Danann

Children of Danu
Kin of the dew
Assembly of gods
Give thanks and laud

Emerged from the mists
Treasures in their midst

Hail to the kings
Sing of the tale
Fate of the sword
Horde of the plate

Sling of the sun
Son of the wing
Cauldron of He
Freedom from Gwyn

Assemble, Emerge
I tremble at thy feet
Power surged
I deny defeat

Tuatha Dé Danann
Aid in this rite
By my words spoken
Come tonight

Greek Deities

Aether

Shivery shield, O winter wind
Wise wielder of air, thick and thin
Bending the breath of Mother Earth
Bringing secrets, bounty, birth

The words to my tongue
Whispers of my calling
Both old and young
Feel pressure falling

Wondrous walls so open, bright
Ancient valleys of blue skies and night

Hidden palace of Arcadia
For fae and creatures alike
Father of Gaia, Earth mother Terra
Azure artist of heavenly sight

Aether skies, fall unto me
I invoke thy sweet serenity

Aphrodite

Sea-born angel
Mermaid Queen
I tread the mill
Of sea-foam green

Walk the shore
Away with me
Show me more
Than eyes can see

Cryptic omen
Coaxing love
Send thy beacon
From heavens above

Aphrodite
Queen of the sea
Aphrodite
I summon thee

From the caverns of ocean floor
From the depths of sailor lore

Goddess of beauty, love & light
Aphrodite, ascend tonight

Let body be mind
And mind be body
Bind this spell
And tie it to me

Athena

Goddess of wisdom
The beat to my drum

Save me from bedlam
Show me to Sanctum

She of a thousand faces
Take me to wondrous places

Journeys far, journeys wide
Path of war, be my guide

Blue eyed Wyld
I am beguiled

Ride the mind
Hide the find

Kingdom old
Kindred new

Truth be told
Mythos too

Let mind's eye choose
My next muse

Ave Agia
Hail Athena

Demeter

Goddess of soil
Fertility rites
As seasons uncoil
We feel thy might

You are the wheel
The cycle, immense
And by thy deal
Winter's offense

Mother and seer
Lordly,
Demeter
I call unto thee

I plant your seed
To set summer free
I treat every weed
As they are dear to me

Hail Demeter
Earthly mother
The drum to my feet
Of soil so sweet

Descend, oh goddess
To our grounded land
Please guide and bless us
Each woman and man

Erebus

King of the Night
Lover of Nyx
Blanket of starlight
And hidden tricks

Weave us thy tapestry
When the Sun Lord slumbers
Silence the majesties
Of lightning and thunder

Erebus
Hear us
Son of Chaos
Be with us

Lord of ancient mystery
God of sweet serenity
As above, so below
Bestow us with thy blackish glow

Grow within our heart and soul
Teach us the way of dark and ole
I walk upon the left hand path
To learn about my darker half

I trace backward the sacred mill
My third eye open
Baptized through the dark moon well
Trance unbroken

Erebus
Hear us
Son of Chaos
Be with us

Gaia

Earth mother wise and bold
Teacher to the ways of old
Of the secrets that shan't be told
Though shown as Autumn's leaves unfold

Dryad hearth & home of Sidhe
Queen of hearts and all that be
Hark our hymn & hark our trance
Heed our hallowed spiral dance

Love and life sustain
Within thy humble acre
By Zeus' rain ye gain
The riddle of thy nature

We cry thy merry name
To the Earth whence we came
To all thine presence known
We hail thy mighty throne

I call thee to our compass
Show us you are with us
Let us experience
And be thy witness

Hekate

Blazing beauty
Shaded shadow
Take us to your bless'd meadow

Charming Champion
Hark our paean
Pagan plea
I call unto thee times three

Hekate, Hekate, Hekate
I prithee, show me the way
Hekate, Hekate, Hekate
Goddess of night and queen to the Day
Hekate, Hekate, Hekate
I prithee, show me the way

Guide of Nighttide
&
Arcane Terrain
Bringer of light and teacher of pain

Travel by crossroad
Call the crow
Hail to the mother of all below

Bide by bone
Ode to the crone
By far and wide thy story known

Reveal your majestic majesty
O' ruler of the divine sanctuary
Lend me your sacred key
Beyond ev'ry tree, grove, glen & mountain
Let us see through your eyes, maiden

Ancient crone, mother, maiden
Awaken

Hypnos

Brother of death
Bringer of peace
Artist of myth,
Magickal beasts

Catcher of dreams
Provider of pleasure
Of starry scenes
And sultry treasures

God of sleep
Father of nightmares
They who reap
From daemon's lair

Oracle of time
Past, present, future
Messages divine
Incubus whisper

Visit me tonight
I invoke thee through my third eye-sight

Bind to me this rite
Ride with me through dreams this night

Nemesis

Blessed is she, the seer of all
Of wrongs and rights
O' Lady of might

Blessed is she, and her sacred law
Advocate of truth
Invoker induce

So I can see, I take thee into me
By the power of three, so mote it be

Lady Nemesis, I call unto thee
Clear the shades of uncertainty

Lady Nemesis, I seek thy decree
I seek thy judging degree

Judge where earthly justice fails
Let truth and light now prevail

Let those who break the Lady's law
Face times three of their victim's fall

Nyx

Born of chaos
Torn from Tartarus
Great mother among us
Hail

First lady of the darkness
Before a moon was ever thought
Possess the imminent
Of later fraught

You are the All Seeing Eye
Where solace is nigh
You are the tapestry
Which cloaks and comforts me

A crone of crones
Reaps her throne
As queen and sire
For all to admire

Our heads we bow
Here and now
To welcome such power
This lavish hour

I call unto the Night
All her grace and might
We make this humble plight
To fulfill this fervent rite

Pan

Gallant, grove stomping
Glorious Pan
Hooves of goat,
Face of man

Through caves untold
Thy mysteries shown
Thy actions bold
As man does groan

You are the sun
And the ground beneath my feet
You are the one
Of verdant vine, rich and sweet

Wise and wond'rous
Holy beast
Pious, righteous
God of feasts

By furtive hand
You take the land

By summer end
Thy will does bend

With ceding grace
Thou plant thy seed
So we may face
The spring thou heed

By the light of faithful flame
I call unto thee by name

By the symbol of sacred birch
My third eye open in eager search

O' mighty, beastly, loving Pan
Take my hand and join back your land

I invite thee to my runic round
I invoke thee by music - spellbound

Thanatos

Hail Thanatos
God of death
God of those
Without their breath

Guide our loved ones home tonight
I invoke thee Thanatos
Show them wherein shadow
There is light

See it their journey safe
No demons faced

Brother of Sleep
Keeper of sheep
Charon treks
Through River Styx
At the crossroads next
To hidden tricks

Point the way
Show our path
The toll I'll pay
To Hades' wrath

By ration of Hades' fruit
I travel that much closer to you
We belong with the dead
Though just tonight you have my head

As sun will rise, so shall I
I'll sever ties and bid goodbye

God of all below
Hail Thanatos

Grigori

Arakiel

Hail the Watchers
Grigori
Fallen

Presence obscure
Glory
Warden

Arakiel, hear me
Keys to the Earth
From land to sea
Bounty and birth

Teach me the signs
The hidden ways
Of great divine
Foregoing days

Teach me sigils
Signs and symbols
Runes of Arakiel
Mental and visual

I invoke thee
Great Grigori
Help me to see
The augury

Armaros

Hail to the Watchers
Grigori
Fallen

Presence obscure
Glory
Warden

Armaros, come forth
In thy ascent
You shall unearth
Grant enchantment

Show me the seals
Permit me the power
And close the deal
This dire hour

Cure & curse
Unhinge & heal
Come, immerse
Show what is real

Teach us to trick
And how to undo
How to be slick
How to break through

Azazel

Hail to the Watchers
Grigori
Fallen

Presence obscure
Glory
Warden

Azazel, prime commander
I invoke your presence
Emanate, lordly leader
Come and fill my senses

He of many faces
Of above and so below
My will he encases
In his steps I will follow

From serpentine roots
To winged flight
From forbidden fruits
To beaconed nights

He of the flame
Fire within
Come put to shame
The bane therein

Baraqel

Hail to the Watchers
Grigori
Fallen

Presence obscure
Glory
Warden

Baraqel, come hither
Be with us now
The sky is your river
By stars, I vow

Teach us of space
The great unknown
Incessant place
Of gods and throne

Fallen star
Grounded guardian
All that you are
Star of Eden

Show me prophecy
All which is fate
And help me foresee
My highest state

Chazaqiel

Hail to the Watchers
Grigori
Fallen

Presence obscure
Glory
Warden

Chazaqiel, arise
Emerge from the fog
In eloquent guise
And astral bog

Teach us of weather
Tales of the mist
Of cloud nymphs and Aether
And why we exist

Send forth your haze
A dreamlike sight
Show us your ways
Of day and the night

Bring your storm
Of thunder and might
Now, take form
In witch's flight

Kokabiel

Hail to the Watchers
Grigori
Fallen

Presence obscure
Glory
Warden

Kokabiel, emerge
From the nether realm
Exalt the scourge
Hymn to Nephilim

Spirit speaker
Summon your aid
I am the seeker
While others, afraid

Break the gates
To the underworld
As I wait
For your power unfurled

I seek guidance
From your domain
Break the silence
Where dead maintain

Penemue

Hail to the Watchers
Grigori
Fallen

Presence obscure
Glory
Warden

Penemue, I invoke you
Angel of knowledge
Come in through
The hidden hedge

Of cryptic language
Obscure, archaic
Angelic vantage
Contour, hypnotic

Secret spells
Spoke and writ
Lost to the well
So man forgets

Forge and form
Banish and bind
Word reform
Text refined

Sariel

Hail to the Watchers
Grigori
Fallen

Presence obscure
Glory
Warden

Sariel, come here and now
Watcher of the moon
In your being I bow
And draw forth your rune

Creature of night
Cast and conjure
Your lunar light
Grandeur & glamour

I draw her down
And bask in her glow
Then look around
And root below

Teach me the secrets
Show me the signs
Reveal the conduit
As the stars align

Shamsiel

Hail to the Watchers
Grigori
Fallen

Presence obscure
Glory
Warden

Shamsiel, shine bright
I invoke thee
Give me sight
Gift me to see

Holy messenger
Keeper of prayer
Keep me from danger
Under your care

Watcher of Eden
Protect my family
Deacon of seasons
Give way to me

Teach of the sun
The map of the sky
So mote it be done
By my mind's eye

Egyptian Deities

Anubis

Noble jackal
Dog of the damned
Hear my call
Our sacred hymn

With sick upon us
We ask your service

Guide our loved ones
See that they pass
And when dead is gone
May memory last

Let souls not linger
But live on forever
And by your holy touch
Our lives are judged

Bring peace, oh Maker
Anubis, Hail
That is your nature
Veracious veil

Bast

Hail the rising sun
The All-Seeing Eye
As children we run
Towards the morning sky

Nightfall stalker
Watching your prey
You are the whisper
Of the huntress way

My war cry echoes
Into the night
Rite of Pharaoh
Feline knight

By the power of three by three by three
Ward away the hungered thieves
I invoke thee, Bastet
Sister of Sekhmet

Accept our libations
Of herbs and potions
A high elation
Of pure emotion

I wish to bind to my familiar
By blood and love I pray
That our link is clear
Synchronized in ancient way

Hathor

Hathor, I bless my altar
In your name
Mother of all
Seen and unseen

I invoke your presence, Hathor
Symbol of beauty and femininity

Please teach us to see
Through your eyes
Teach us to be
One with the sky

May I allure the one I seek
With music of my heart
And may their heart I keep
So that we never part

Horus

God of the sky
All Seeing Eye
Ancient protector
Whom all adore

Son of Isis
Prodigy of Osiris
Come from hiding
Behind her wing

Defeat the evil
I say by name:

_____

Keep him until
He owns his shame

Let righteousness rule
Let light prevail
Contain the cruel
Beneath the veil

Horus, come to us
Horus, guide us
To which is just
Through love and trust

Horus, be among us

Isis

Holy Hent
Serpent Queen
Kind and keen
As any king

Daughter of Sky and Earth
Mother and giver of birth

Loyal wife
Oracle too
Bringer of life
Taker too

By side of Osiris she does rule
Above and below she does protect
From Ra and Set and those who're cruel
She awes her people and gains respect

Among the greats
The ancient five
Foes ablate
She does thrive

Sacred Isis
Be among us

Osiris

Beloved of Isis
Murder unjust
Murdock the lawless
Slay Her trust

Piece by piece
His body found
All pain released
And soul Earthbound

Great Osiris, be among us
Fair and righteous
Ominous king
Welcome all the light you bring

As above and so below
From first breath to final blow

Keeper of the underworld
Watcher of all life unfurled

I call you home
To physical form
Free from your tomb
The nether storm

Sekhmet

Goddess of magic and infinite power
A tempest flows through the veins of the Earth
And is a testament of willpower
But a truth that I discern

Sekhmet of the sands
Of the storms that lay to waste
The eldest of the lands
I call to you with haste

As like the lion, I roar
In your image
And like a titan of war
In your visage

I show you here and now I'm worthy
To face any adversary
That the issue is more than worldly
That I confirm with certainty

I'm in need of your divinity
Sekhmet, come to me

Thoth

God of magic
God of wisdom
God of ancient hieroglyphics
Hail from your mighty kingdom

Head of ibis
Aid to Isis
By potent compass
Be among us

We bow to your divinity
We worship all your charity

Scribe of ancient theory
Cipher lore and mystery
Write through me so I may see
All that was and is and be

With the virtue of new-found sight
Keep the balance of dark and light

King of mystics, much adept
Liberate thy knowledge kept

Hindu Deities

Brahma

Holy creator
Universal lord
Mighty savior
So loved and adored

God of infinity
Knowledge adept
Sacred trinity
Of secrets kept

I supplicate your wit
Your patience as writ
You are my mantra
Brahma

Ganapati

Atman and Maya
You are soul
Son of Shiva
You are whole

Leader of Bhutaganas, hail
Torn and tattered, Ganesha
Fighting strong, each thrash and flail
End the rite by *pradakshina*

Broken tusk
Endurance high
Do what you must
And dignify

God of obstacles
Small and large
Slay and cull
And take your charge

Ganapati
I invoke thee
Pradakshina
Ganesha

Kali

Daunting flower
Midnight queen
Endless power
You are a dream

She of time,
Change,
Death

I walk your path
In every breath

Kali, come to me
Mighty, beastly
Fearsome, Kali

Stand by me
Midst the enemy

Indulge in wine,
Flesh and power
On this divine,
Magick hour

MahaKali
Arms of plenty
Show to me
Your brilliancy

Saraswati

Goddess of knowledge
Music and words
Saraswati, I pledge
Swear and begird

Mother of Vedas
Be among us

Flow of ink to paper
Sway of gentle river

Wife of Brahma
I invoke you
Varada mudra
I gift you

Shiva

Shiva of the *trimurti*
Ancient protector
Deviant, beastly
In archaic lore

He leads the tendrils of darkness
Of duress and fearful sprites
In spite of goodness and might
He rules the night

Creator of demons
Monsters and fright
As love was gone
Burned; benight

Chaos was cast
Darkness spread
And Bhutaganas
Took their heads

Heed the *Linga*
His grace and might
I invoke Shiva
The king of night

Vishnu

Avatar of *dharma*
God of luxury
Enforcer of karma
He of the three

Hero of epics
Of many faces
Holy, ancient
Of many graces

Immortality
Divine discovery
By the power of three
Vishnu, come to me

Mesopotamian Deities

Anu

God of the heavens
Dominion of sky
He is the High One
Beginning of time

Father of many
Ruler of all
Giver of plenty
Please hear my call

Come to us Anu
Accept my prayer
You're the one that I call to
Great god of air

Cryptic,
Wise Ancient
Of spirits and stars
Fix and eclipse
The pain in our hearts

Enki

Son of Anu
He of *Apsû*

Master plan
Craftsman

Show us a sign

God of the gardens, the land and the sea
Come down upon us and help us to see

Humble, pious
Splendid, righteous

Though tempted
Lured from

The treach'rous divide

He is a creator
A skillful one
Of great tales and lore
Known to everyone

Enlil

Flood bringer
Harbinger

He of the three
And of destiny

Ruler and lord
Lost, he repents
In the Underworld
Where he was sent

Father of the Moon
Hunting and War
Of the runic round
And roar of the night

Great Enlil
Help me to be
Help me to feel
The power of three

Give us sight
To what future holds
Bless our rite
With power bold

Inanna

Daughter of love and skies
Sweet songs & lullabies
Prowling lioness
Loyal goddess

Names of many
Ishtar, Astarte, Aphrodite
All in one, I call unto thee

I honor your bravery
Desire & intensity
Time altered journey
Of strain and fertility

Your Underworld travels
We honor each season
As days unravel
You are our reason

I invoke thee Inanna
Into my compass
Isis, Diana
Become among us

Lilith

Enchantress of the garden
First lady of Eden
Divine feminine
Embodied of sin

I drink to thy courage
And I praise for thy wits
I bow to thy prestige
So mote it be as writ'

Hail Lilith
Darkened Queen
Please visit
In my dreams

I am thy student
Thy loyal devotee
By no accident,
Am I bound to thee

Goddess of lust, war & pain
We tremble at thy mighty reins
I am taken by thy ebon wing
I am shaken by the sway thou bring

Grace us with thy visage
Wherein our earthly realm
I work in thy image
Honored martyr of Hell

Lucifer

Forsaken angel
Bringer of light
Cast to darkness
Stripped of flight

Since thou fell
Thy reputation
Is that of Hell
Those of imitation

Curse thy name
With honor vain
Make evil same
As unjust reign

Faith is nigh
On hopeless nights
So show a sign
To me tonight

Nabu

God over wisdom
And oracle
Of spells and rhythms
So wonderful

Known to the people
Under many o'names
We carry your will
And keep up the flame

Hail Nabu
All that you do

Please share your secrets
Let us not forget

I invoke you, Nabu
And all that you knew

Tiamat

Tiamat, the wind to my breath
You are the Heavens
You are the Earth
Goddess of death
Goddess of birth

Born of chaos
Creator, I bow to you
Please join us
Drink with us our witch's brew

Accept libations
Of salt and blood
Come to land again
With cleansing flood

Your sacrifice we honor
Our devotion we offer

Lady Chaos
Lady Darkness
Please join us

From salt to water
From warmth to fire
As above, below and in between
Goddess rise, so mote it be

Miscellaneous

Ancestors

I call to my bloodline
My sacred fire
With the aid of my shrine
May barrier shatter

Between then and now
What was and is
The time enow
It is my wish

I set libation
For your peace
And hope you'll listen
To my plea

Take form, beloved _____
Help is needed
From eyes of the dead

Travel Styx, Charon reverse
Take away the silence
Of Dead Man's Curse
And sleep immense

I prithee peace
I prithee well
Now release
From the spirit well

Fae

Gifts rich & sweet
Of milk & honey
A fitting treat
To call the faeries

Watch thy step
Don't even blink
Where the river ebbs
The Fae dost drink

Come and sing
An old folk song
Dance & bring
Your friends along

I ask to play
Beside the Fae
By and by
Where faeries fly

Spirit of the Departed

_____ (Say their full name)

In life I knew you
In death, I still do

_____ (Say their full name)

Come forth to me
I invite you here and now
My energy
Is yours to borrow for now

I invoke your presence here
In the physical world
We are passed the point of tears
To exchange final words

Leave the penumbra
I'll be your medium

_____ (Say their full name)

Spirit Guide

Spirit guide
I call ye hence
I sing your name
Raise my defenses

_____ (Speak their name)

Praise be unto thee
Walk with me
The path of dreams
Of the unseen
Anomalies

_____ (Speak their name)

I invoke thee here and now
As long as thee allow

Nordic Deities

Aegir

Spirit of water
River of flesh
Refresh when hotter
God of the west

With morning dew
Upon sacred yew
The synergy,
Ley-line symphony

From water and vine
To succulent wine
Wash and bury
The secrets I carry
Lord of the sea
Primal selkie

From sandy beach
To hillside reach
I call unto thee

Splash your waters
Upon my altar
Unto me

Unstoppable tide
O' blessed seaside
Crash your waves

Flow and lave
Guide and weave
Send relief

I invoke thy divine fav'r
O' fervent savior

I await thy high command
And thy demand

I call to the Lake
I call to the Sea
I call ye to take
My sorrow from me

Freya

Aesir Lady
Fragile Darkness
I call to ye
And your finesse

Queen of the field
Fólkvangr
Where souls are sealed
Sessrúmnir

Seidr incantations
Trick of the tongue
Be of concentration
Stray from the sun

Goddess o' mystery
Hail, O' *völva*
She of wizardry
I call unto ye, Freya

Logi

Warm the heart
Warm the soul
Tear apart
The fears I hold

Lord of the flame
My humble liege
I call your name
And power siege

Grant me courage
Grant me power
To fight the scourge
This magick hour

Mighty Logi, I call upon thee
Light thy flame so I may see

Lend me fire
So I may fight
When time is dire
There is no light

Scorching spirit
Sacred Fire
With thy permit
I claim thy power

Loki

Father of Hel
Trickster of ol'
By timeworn spell
I pray for my soul

For self is the key
But selfishness waits
With misery,
Death and decay

Let struggle and hardship
Be cast away
Let the foolish slip
And cast to grey

I ask for endurance
Courage and vigor
As well as severance
And fear nevermore

Loki, I summon ye
Your knot of faith
To have security
Until the end of days

Odin

God of penance
Dexterous deity
I mimic the war dance
Of victory

One-eyed wonder
Dynamic, Odin
Kill and sunder
The fear within

Writer, poet
Warrior too
Always outwit
Contending fools

Antediluvian
Odin, I invoke ye
Of strong obsidian
And gentle tree

I call for your might
Your will to fight
A witty end
And war amend

Thor

Great giant slayer
Booming storm
Wielder of *Mjollnir*
A tool of reform

I call to Thor
Your bravery
Your mighty roar
Of blood-drenched fury

I ask for strength
This solemn hour
And at arm's length
Your grisly power

Mighty Thor
Strike your hammer
I implore
The end to war

Serpentine battle
World spinner
May death not rattle
May we claim winner

Roman Deities

Bacchus

Wyld seeker
Of youth and grove
Satyr leader

Fiery kiss
Fill now my void
By your thyrsus
Doubt destroyed

Tall and mighty
God of the vine
Rigid and beastly
The world is thine

I gift thee honey
Ivy and wine
Grant me money
Abundance, divine

Hail Bacchus
I call thee forth
Be among us!
Rise from the Earth

Ceres

Goddess of harvest
Of fruit and grain
Autumn artist
Prosp'rous gain

Come Ceres
I call thee hence
From Hades
Magick, commence

As you spin the wheel
Seasons do change
I break your seal
Light exchange

He who sows
May also reap
He who owes
His soul I'll keep

If his intent
May vex my family
I'll not relent
And hex him, happily

Diana

As the moon doth shine
She does wait
Drinking wine
Wading the lake

I am a daughter of darkness
Serving the light
The mists of the waters
Dance with the moonlight
As sunlight doth falter
I am a star in the night
I will face the fight

Mother of the poor
The weak and wicked
Open thy door
To which is predicted

Hail Diana
I invoke thee
Grand arcana
Holy Witch Queen

By the croak of the frog
Make thyself known
By the howl from the dog
Make presence shown

Luna

Crescent captor
White horned bull
Necromancer
Leyline pull

Moon incarnate
Luna! Hail!
Night-tide spirit
Starry Veil

Mystic mother
Clever crone
Come and gather
By bone and stone

I invoke the light of the round
Draw down thy rapture
As the howls of the hound doth sound
Witches do gather

Luna, I invoke thee
The magick of the night
And with great certainty,
I draw to me, your light

Terra

Earth dwelling Lady
I bring ye my oath
Each green and daisy
I promise ye growth

The Earth is our home
She is our mother
And within this dome
I will discover

The song of the trees
The drums of the dirt
The hum of the bees
The wind through my shirt

Bringer of life
I call ye hence!
By songbird fife
And rose incense

I call the thorn
I call the flower
By faerie horn
This fateful hour

Bless this child
Make her of nature
Let her wyld
Instincts tame her

Give her beauty
Like Terra herself
With smile, lovely
And make her wealthy

May this child never know hardship
May the faeries keep eyes
May this child enjoy her kinship
And spread truth, not lies

Terra, Earth Mother,
I call ye hence
I call forth thunder
Let life commence

Venus

Shape of us
Hail Venus

Desire
Power
Come feed us

Shower me with love
Gift me grace like a dove
And when the morning comes
Make the Night succumb

Presence
Intense
Do not
Relent
Do not
Repent

Venus I invoke thee
Your teachings of amity
Grant your light upon me
Cure me from my misery

May I find love, peace and happiness
I swear to thee upon my breast
I give the true me, as I undress
Naked before thee, I will confess

In return, for secrets told
I ask of thee to make me bold

Let heads turn over
When I pass by
Neck over shoulder
Let feelings fly
Let the right ones come to me
In the name of Venus, so mote it be

Vesta

The heart
The hearth
The home
Vesta

The home goddess of Rome,
Vesta

We pave
We play
We praise
Vesta

Our family's hearts & souls
Vesta

Kindle
Cradle
Comfort
Vesta

I invoke ye here and now
Vesta

Saints

Saint Anthony

Praise be, Saint Anthony
Bring back what belongs to me
For it is my property
And it's stuck in purgatory

In the name of all that is holy
And all that is to be
Bring my possessions back to me

Saint Anthony, I invoke thee
Patron of lost things

Manifest the missing
I thank thee for thy blessings
Thy presence
And guidance
All the hope you bring us

Saint Christopher

Weight heavy on my back
The days and weeks do blend
Weakness at my feet
And hardship on my hands

Saint Christopher, I call to thee
I summon your presence here to me

These burdens that I carry
I long to bury

I'm working for my family
To have food to eat

But everything lately
Just seems too heavy

If you take some weight from me
I promise to gift thee greatly

Saint Expedite

I break cake with thee
Share red rose & wine
These libations are thine
Please come to me

Ribbons of red, gold and green
HODIE, HODIE, HODIE
So mote it be
Thy delivery timely
And my payment have not delay

Saint Expeditus
Be among us
For I'm in crisis
And need thy guidance

For these urgent matters I petition
Set haze to my intuition

I ask that they be taken care of
In the name of the Lord and heavens above

Saint Joseph

I wish for work
An honest living
To give birth to
This hopeful wishing

Saint Joseph, I invoke thee
By sigil on my talisman
The force of change calls unto me
With whispers of God's plan

I seek out employment
A chance at fortune
Or meager enjoyment
A life to live in

Determined am I
To find a title
I will not die
A peasant's battle

Saint Lazarus

I wish to speak
To those who can't
Whose tongues are shriveled
By the curse of death

Give them words this fateful hour
Grace them with your miracles—
Your power

Saint Lazarus, I call you here
Hear me now, loud and clear

Show me the soul
Show me the spirit
Make them whole
As holy writ

Bring _____ here with us
But bless them by the cross
I entrust thee, Lazarus
To bring them here across

And when we exchange words
Return them to their world
Whether it be heaven or hell,
I will not beg thee tell

And by the sound of the bell
May it be the death knell

To return _____ to sleep
In eternal peace

San Alejo

San Alejo, I beg thy strength
In virtue, stamina and willpower
There are those that wish me pain
To see me suffer

But under thy protection
I will never succumb
To the demons in the reflection
To whom they wish I become

San Alejo, I beg thee here and now
My enemies marked by candle
With my power I endow
To ward away evil

Santa Muerte

Santa Muerte
I ask for healing
For direction
And abundance

Santa Muerte
Walk with the living
With affection
Come join my dance

Lady of death, I honor you
An effigy set in your name
Until I'm dust, I pay my dues
And I decree by candle flame

Santa Muerte
My goddess
My witness
My intentions are pure

Santa Muerte
Grant my favor
And my word is yours

Shinto

Amaterasu

Amaterasu,
Kami-Sama
Great goddess,
Dainichi Buddha

Glowing, radiant
She of the sun
Splendid, brilliant
The shining one

Takama no Hara
Of long ago
Kaji ga shinda
Ama-no-Iwato

Hyō no Amaterasu,
Bring back your light
I call unto you
To aid this rite

Izanagi

Kami of creation
He who walks beyond the pillar
And by my libation
I walk the path of a stranger

Izanagi, come forth
I ask to walk along *Yomi*
At the end of the Earth
And from his clutches, please spare me

Love is infinite
Both alive and dead
Simple, intricate
I hold my breath

Let me walk
Beside the lifeless
Where dead talk
And we are timeless

Izanami

Loving sister
Shining jewel
Star-crossed lovers
United you rule

I cross the bridge
Between life and death
Let my loved one live
Let him keep his breath

Hail Kami
Shinigami

Lift the gates
Here I wait

Anata o yobimasu
Izanami-*sama*
I invoke you

Shichi-Fuku-Jin

I call upon prosperity
Fortune and luck
I call upon bravery
May I be struck

With love and wealth
And perfect health

Abundance
A cup that never empties
Guidance
A purpose and expertise

Shichi-Fuku-Jin
Here and now, I invite you in
And I vow, to praise the seven

Nana, Hyo! Nana, Hyo!
Yumi O! Yumi O!
Shichi-*Sama*
Hear me, *ima*!

Shichi-Fuku-Jin
The seven wonders
I pray that you bring
Wisdom and answers

Susanoo

Guide my actions
Let me prevail
Come forth; ascend
And you, I'll hail

Susanoo, *Hyo*!
Say it be so

Help me slay
The dragons around me
Blessed melee
Kusanagi

Sharpen my edges
Tear down my bounds
Ride on the hedges
And strike them down

Susanoo-*Sama*
I evoke you and your will
Rakasha
Come get your fill

Tsukiyomi

Light of the night
Tsukiyomi
Glorious light
Ore wa hitori janai

Keep me warm
Hoshizora no yume
Calm the storm
Fukai basho de

I call down your light
Cast it upon me
King of the Night!
Praise Tsuki!

Slavic

Belobog—Chernobog

White candle lit
On the table in the hearth
Black candle lit
Together but apart

Belobog of light
I invoke you here tonight

Chernobog of night
Balance out the light

Give me good and evil
Or neither of the two
I know both are needed
For balance to be true

Lada

Lada, bless the bride
So she may live life long
Lada, bless the groom
So he may do no wrong
Lada of the Spring
Blessing everything
Lada, bless this wedding
With love and offering

Lada, I invite you
To sing and dance with us
Join merry, and *przyjęcie*
And make this union true

Marzanna

From the harsh kiss of winter
Marzanna, we make way
We pray thanks to Her
In hopes of sunny days

I invoke you, Marzanna
I beckon at the river
I dress the copse with *sosna*
So bounty you'll deliver

Mokosh

Bless this seed
This fruit
This flower

By abounding breasts
And my divine altar

Mokosh, I invoke you
For blessings upon this womb
By this flowery wash
And censering this room

Bless it for a child
So they may grow in grace
May their smile beguile
All whom gaze their face

Perun

From the highest branches
Of the grand Oak
The god of the witches
The sword of stone

Perun, grant me your power
Perun, share your thunder
I invoke you through my scepter
The devil's finger

Reveal the golden apple
With a burning arrow through it
A treasure one cannot steal
Without disease at one's heel

A bite for me will heal a curse
But a taste from another will do its worst

Perun, show me lightening
Great ruler of the living

See my humble sacrifice
And grant me your light tonight

Triglav

Heaven, Earth, Hell
Prav, Yav, Nav
Air, Water, Soil
Prav, Yav, Nav

I summon you here, Triglav
The breeze, the trees, the sea
Three faces come to be
In my vision, mote it be

Zorya

She of the morning star
Open heaven's gates
Brightest one afar
I invoke you to this place

She of the Evening Star
Open twilight's gates
Shimmering sister
I invoke you to this place

She of the Midnight Star
Open the night's gates
Darkest sister
I invoke you to this place

Zorya of balance
Of trials
Come in three

Zorya of chaos
And goodness
Come enlighten me

Made in the USA
Columbia, SC
24 June 2022